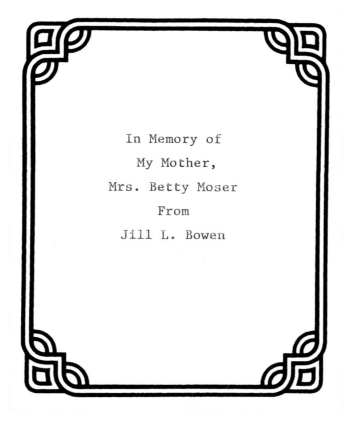

In Memory of
My Mother,
Mrs. Betty Moser
From
Jill L. Bowen

Why Why Why were the pyramids built?

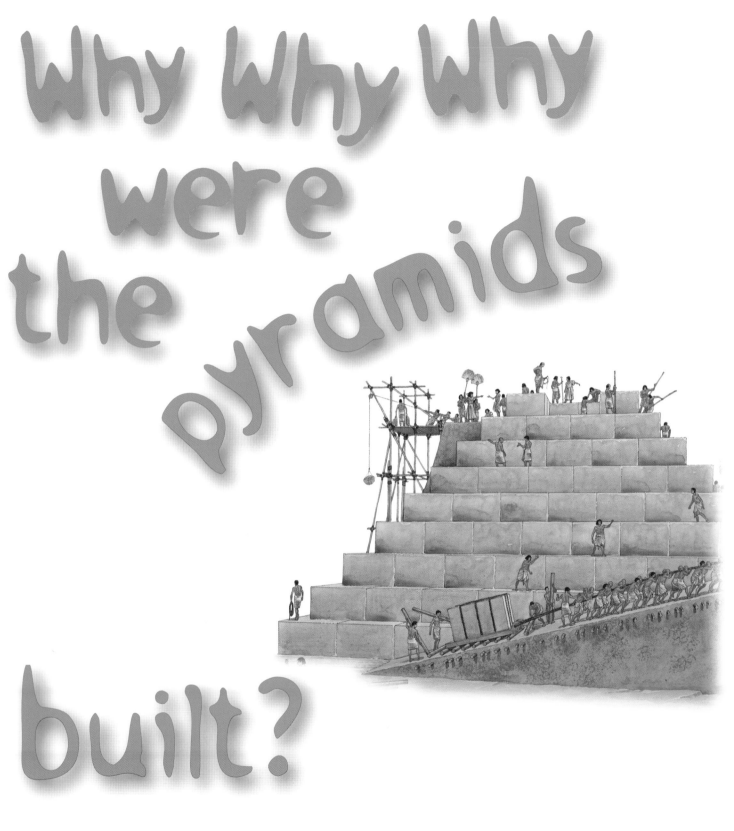

First published as hardback in 2006 by
Miles Kelly Publishing Ltd, Bardfield Centre,
Great Bardfield, Essex, CM7 4SLCopyright
© Miles Kelly Publishing Ltd 2006

This 2009 edition published and distributed
by:

Mason Crest Publishers Inc.
370 Reed Road, Broomall, Pennsylvania
19008
(866) MCP-BOOK (toll free)
www.masoncrest.com

Why Why Why—
Were the Pyramids Built?
ISBN 978-1-4222-1590-6
Library of Congress Cataloging-in-
Publication data is available

Why Why Why—?
Complete 23 Title Series
ISBN 978-1-4222-1568-5

Printed in the United States of America

Contents

Why were the pyramids built?

Pyramids were tombs (burial places) for Egyptian rulers, called pharaohs. The three great pyramids of Khufu, Khafre and Menkaure were built in Giza, Egypt, 4500 years ago. The Great Pyramid of Khufu is the biggest. It took 20 years and 4000 workers to build it!

Great Pyramid of Pharaoh Khufu

Pyramid of Pharaoh Khafre

Pyramid of Pharaoh Menkaure

What guards the Great Pyramid?

The pyramids were full of treasures. A stone statue was built to guard the Great Pyramid at Giza. It was carved in the shape of a sphinx. A sphinx has the body of a lion and the head of a man. The sphinx at the Great Pyramid has the face of Pharaoh Khafre.

The sphinx

Tomb robbers!

'The Book of Buried Pearls' told robbers all about the treasures inside the tombs. It also showed them how to get past spirits that guarded the dead.

What was inside the Great Pyramid?

The Great Pyramid had two huge burial chambers. They were built for the pharaoh and his queen. A corridor called the Grand Gallery led to the pharaoh's chamber. The corridor's ceiling was 26 feet tall!

Map

Draw a plan of a pyramid. Include secret tunnels and hidden rooms to stop the robbers.

Who was the top god?

Ancient Egyptians worshipped more than 1000 gods. The most important was Ra, the Sun god. Every evening, Ra was swallowed by Nut, the sky goddess. At night, Ra travelled through the land of the dead. He was born again each morning. Later, Ra became Amun Ra, king of the gods.

Ra →

Dead body god!

Anubis was the god in charge of dead bodies. He looked like a jackal, a kind of dog. People who wrapped bodies for burial often wore Anubis masks!

Why were cats important?

Cats were sacred (holy) animals in ancient Egypt. The goddess for cats, musicians and dancers was called Bastet. When a pet cat died it was wrapped up carefully and placed in a special cat-shaped coffin. Then the cat was buried in a cat cemetery!

Who took care of the temples?

Fabulous temples were built for the gods. Many temples were built for Amun Ra, king of the gods. Priests looked after the temples, their riches and the lands around them. These massive statues of Pharaoh Ramses II guard the temple at Abu Simbel.

Draw

Draw a picture of Ra travelling through the night in the land of the dead. He travelled in a boat.

Temple at Abu Simbel

Which queen found a magical land?

Queen Hatshepsut sent explorers to look for Punt, a magical land she had heard about. Punt was said to be filled with treasure and animals. The explorers returned with gold, ivory, perfumes and special oils. In fact, Punt was probably part of present-day Somalia in Africa.

Shaving for the gods!

Ancient Egyptians could only visit temples for the gods if they shaved off their hair and eyebrows!

Who was the boy king?

Tutankhamun became king of Egypt when he was just nine years old. He was just 18 years old when he died. His tomb was discovered in 1922. Inside was a solid gold death mask of the king.

Death mask of Tutankhamun

Queen Hatshepsut

Make

Find six boxes that fit inside each other. Decorate them with things a pharaoh might use in the next world.

What did tomb robbers find?

Ancient Egyptian kings were buried with all the things they might need in the world of the dead. These included gold, silver, jewels, furniture and even cooking pots. Robbers stole the lot – even the bodies! But robbers did not find King Tutankhamun's tomb.

How were the pyramids built?

Thousands of workers had to cut blocks of stone to the right shape using chisels and saws. Wooden sledges were then used to drag the stones to the pyramid. Each stone weighed more than two and a half big elephants!

Finished pyramid

Wooden sledge for dragging blocks

Busy busy!
One ancient Egyptian was a very busy man! Imhotep was a doctor, a priest and a poet. He also designed and built a pyramid!

The pharaoh checked the work

Were the pyramids painted white?

The finished pyramids had a bright white coating. This wasn't paint, but limestone, which protected the stones beneath. Inner walls were built from clay bricks that were lined with pink granite. White stone covered the floors.

Teams of workers dragged the stones up slopes

How did the workers build so high?

The stones were pulled up a ramp to get to each level of the pyramid. The ramp was a steep slope made from baked earth bricks. The pyramid got higher and higher. So the ramp had to be made longer and longer! Sledges were pulled up the ramp on rollers.

Think

Look at the walls and ceilings of your house. What do you think they were built with?

How do you make a mummy?

Ancient Egyptians mummified their dead. First, the inside parts such as the brain, but not the heart, were removed. Then the body was salted and dried. Cloth was stuffed inside the body to help it keep its shape. Then the body was oiled and wrapped in lots of bandages.

Mummy case

All wrapped up!

The mummy was wrapped in tight bandages. This helped to stop the body from rotting away.

The priest in charge

Mummy

Make

Cut out a mummy mask from card and paint it with a face. It could be the face of an animal.

What did the priest do?

The priest sent the dead person's spirit into the next world. He touched parts of the body with special instruments. This was so that the body could move around in the world of the dead. The mouth could speak and eat in its new life after being touched!

What were mummies kept in?

The mummy was placed in a case. Some cases were just wooden boxes. Others were beautifully decorated. An important person, such as a pharaoh, was placed in a stone coffin called a sarcophagus (sarc-off-a-gus).

Sarcophagus (sarc-off-a-gus)

Did Egypt have an army?

Ancient Egypt had a powerful army that won many battles. About 3500 years ago, the Egyptians made a new weapon. It was a chariot pulled by two horses and driven by two soldiers. They drove very fast at the enemy and fired arrows at them.

Chariot

Who defeated Egypt?

General Ptolemy defeated Egypt over 2300 years ago. The rulers who followed him were called the Ptolemies. They built a new city called Alexandria. It was guarded by a massive lighthouse. The city also had a museum and a huge library with thousands of books.

Buzz off!

Egyptian soldiers were given golden fly medals! Perhaps it's because the soldiers annoyed the enemy so much!

Warship

Who were the Sea People?

The Sea People attacked Egypt and tried to take over the country. Pharaoh Ramses III sent lots of warships to try to defeat them. The ships had sails and oars for travelling quickly at sea. The Sea People were beaten back by the Egyptians.

Read

Can you remember what new weapon the Egyptians made? Read the pages again to remind you.

15

What did the Egyptians sell?

In ancient Egypt, people did not use money to buy things. They exchanged things with other people. This was called bartering. Egypt's best goods for bartering were gold and cattle. They also traded paper, which was made from papyrus, a grass-like plant.

List

Make a list of the goods that ancient Egyptians exchanged. What do you think they were used for?

Was Egypt very rich?

There were gold mines in the deserts of Egypt. The gold made Egypt very rich. In fact Egypt was the richest country in the ancient world.

Zap!

Giraffe tails were brought to Egypt from Africa. They were used as fly swatters!

What did the Egyptians buy?

The Egyptians held big markets where they could buy or exchange all kinds of things. Special oils, wood and animals were very popular. People also bought jewelry that was made from a precious stone called lapis lazuli.

Did food grow in the desert?

Most of Egypt was in the hot desert. However, every year in July, the great river Nile flooded the dry fields. The water brought rich, black soil with it. This soil spread in wide strips on each side of the river. Farmers sowed their seed in this good soil.

Cattle were counted

How did the Egyptians farm?

Farmers used oxen and wooden plows to dig the soil. They weeded and dug channels with hoes. Then they planted seed, mostly by hand. Farmers also kept goats, sheep, ducks and geese. They kept bees to make honey.

Farmers' crops

What did farmers grow?

Farmers grew barley for beer and grapes for wine. Dates, figs, melons, cucumbers, onions, leeks and lettuces grew well in the rich soil. Wheat was also grown to make bread.

Farm workers

Draw

Draw a basket full of crops grown by Egyptian farmers. You can see an Egyptian basket in this picture.

Water from the river Nile

Who had the best jobs?

Doctors, high priests or priestesses and government officers had the best jobs.

So did viziers. A vizier helped the pharaoh to rule the land. Next came the traders and craftsmen, such as carpenters and jewelers. Laborers and farmhands had the poorest jobs.

Who was head of the family?

In ancient Egypt the man was the head of the family. The eldest son was given all the land, property and riches when his father died. Women could also own land and property and get good jobs.

Little monkey!

Pet baboons were sometimes trained to climb fig trees and pick the ripe fruit!

Children playing

Vizier checking grain

What did children play with?

Children played with toys made from clay and wood. They had carved animals with legs and heads that could move. They also had spinning tops, clay balls, toy horses and dolls. Children played games such as leapfrog and tug-of-war, too.

Imagine

Imagine you are an Egyptian worker. Which job would you choose to do and why?

Who had the biggest houses?

Rich Egyptians lived in large country houses called villas.

Villas often had several storys. Some had walled gardens with fruit orchards and a fish pond. Poor families often lived in one room. Many lived on crowded streets in the towns and cities.

Rich family

How did the Egyptians cook?

Some ancient Egyptians cooked their food in a clay oven. Others cooked on an open fire. Clay ovens were made from baked clay bricks. Wood or charcoal were burned as fuel. Cooks used pottery saucepans with two handles.

Mud and straw mixture was poured into a wooden frame

Finished bricks

Were houses built with bricks?

Egyptian houses were built with bricks. Mud from the river Nile was mixed with straw and pebbles. The mixture was shaped into brick shapes and dried in the hot sun. Trunks from palm trees held up the flat roofs. Inside walls were plastered and painted.

Make

Mix clay with dried grass and pebbles. Put the mixture in an ice-cube tray. Let your bricks dry in the sun.

Sticky fingers!

Ancient Egyptians ate with their fingers. Rich people washed their hands between each dish. Their servants brought jugs of washing water for them.

Who shaved their hair off?

Both men and women shaved their hair off. They believed that this kept them clean. Men and women also wore make-up such as black kohl, which lined their eyes. Fingernail paint and face powder were also used. Red coloring was worn on lips and cheeks.

Egyptian lady

Cosy toes!

Rich people wore shoes made with padded leather. Sandals were made of the grass-like papyrus plant. Poor people went barefoot.

Did Egyptians ever wear wigs?

Rich Egyptians wore wigs made from human hair or sheep's wool. The wigs were kept in boxes held on stands. Egyptians also used hair dye. Girls plaited their hair into pigtails. Some boys wore a pigtail on one side.

Wigs

Ivory comb

Wooden comb

Hair pins

What was the fashion?

Rich women wore the best linen cloth with beads sewn onto it. The cloth was dyed in pale colors. It was made into long dresses and cloaks. Men wore long robes. They also wore cloths wrapped around the waist. These were tied in a knot.

Make

Draw an Egyptian wearing clothes and make-up. Use wool to make a wig. Glue this to the person's head.

Who were the workers?

Most Egyptians were laborers who worked on farms and building sites. There were also carpenters, potters, jewelers and shoemakers. These people were called craftworkers and they had shops in towns. Some worked for rich people.

Craftworker

Draw

Draw symbols for different jobs. Try a hammer for a carpenter or a ring for a jeweler.

How did Egyptians write?

Egyptians used symbols for writing. These were called hieroglyphs. Some hieroglyphs stood for words. Others stood for sounds. School children had to learn 700 different hieroglyphs!

School children

Did people write on paper?

The Egyptians had no paper. Instead they wrote on papyrus. This was made from reeds that grew next to the river Nile. Papyrus lasts a long time. Sheets of it have survived 3,000 years!

Packed lunch!

Workers took bread, onions and a cucumber for their lunch. They washed it down with weak beer.

Who decorated the tombs?

Artists decorated the inside walls of tombs with bright paintings. They painted scenes from the dead person's life. The person always looked young and healthy in the pictures! Egyptians thought that the pictures would come to life in the land of the dead.

Hieroglyphs

Scary smell!

Strong-smelling garlic was used to scare away snakes. It also got rid of long tapeworms inside people's stomachs!

What could doctors do?

Doctor

Egyptian doctors knew how the body worked. They could even mend broken bones by setting them. Doctors could also treat fevers. They used medicines made from plants such as garlic and juniper. Juniper is a bush with sweet-smelling berries.

Did Egyptians study the stars?

People called astronomers studied the movement of the stars. Sirius was the brightest and most important star. The movement of Sirius was used to create the Egyptian calendar. Egyptians used astronomy to build temples in line with the Sun or a star.

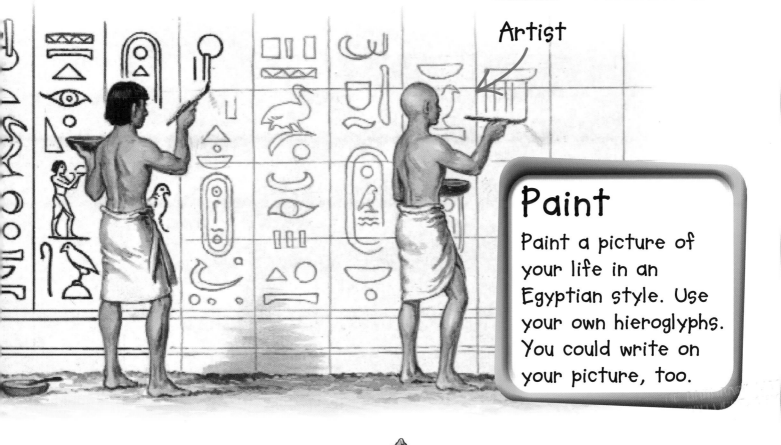

Artist

Paint

Paint a picture of your life in an Egyptian style. Use your own hieroglyphs. You could write on your picture, too.

Quiz time

Do you remember what you have read about Egypt? These questions will test your memory. The pictures will help you. If you get stuck, read the pages again.

3. Who was the boy king?

page 9

4. Which queen found a magical land?

page 8

page 5

1. What guards the Great Pyramid?

5. What were mummies kept in?

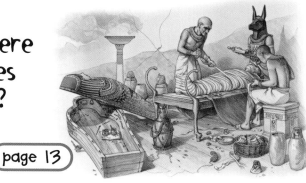

page 13

page 7

2. Why were cats important?

6. Who defeated Egypt?

page 14

7. What did farmers grow?

page 19

11. Who shaved their hair off?

page 24

page 20

8. Who was head of the family?

12. What was the fashion?

page 25

13. How did Egyptians write?

page 27

9. What did children play with?

page 21

10. How did the Egyptians cook?

page 22

Answers

1. The sphinx
2. Because they were holy
3. Tutankhamun
4. Hatshepsut
5. Mummy case or sarcophagus
6. General Ptolemy
7. Barley, grapes, dates, figs, melons, cucumbers, onions, leeks and lettuces
8. The man
9. Wooden or clay toys, spinning tops, clay balls, toy horses and dolls
10. With clay ovens or open fires
11. Men and women
12. Dresses, cloaks and long robes
13. With hieroglyphs

Index